I0199418

EVERYBODY
TOOTS

Copyright © 2018 by Cori Nevruz
All rights reserved.
All illustrated characters are fictitious and are not based on real people.
This book or any portion thereof may not be reproduced or used in any manner whatsoever
without the express written permission of the author except for the use of brief quotations in a book review.

First Printing, 2018

Everybody Toots!

That means YOU.

Everybody Toots!

That means me, too.

Everybody Toots!

Your mommy and dad;

Everybody Toots!

Your doggy and cat.

Everybody Toots!

Your grandpa toots a lot.

Everybody Toots!

The lady in the barber shop.

Everybody Toots!

Your grade school teacher;

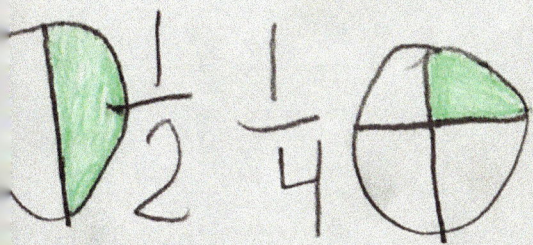

Everybody Toots!

Your pastor and your preacher.

Everybody Toots!

The big football player;

Fart!

Fart

Everybody Toots!

The president and the mayor.

Everybody Toots!

The firefighter at the station;

Everybody Toots!

The doctor's office patient.

Everybody Toots!

The fellow who drives your bus;

Everybody Toots!

So, what does that mean to us?

EVERYBODY TOOTS

www.ingramcontent.com/pod-product-compliance
Lightning Source LLC
Chambersburg PA
CBHW050638150426
42811CB00053B/993